Young Actors
Plays for drama students aged 11-15

Chris Jones

Copyright © 2022 Chris Jones

All rights reserved.

ISBN: 9798360822066

DEDICATION

This book is dedicated to Amy, Annie, Charis, Eriskay, Esther, Hollie, Imogen, Isabella, Jasmine, Jasper, Jemima, Lily, Max, Molly, Noah, Rio, Seb, Shona, Thomas, Tommy, Toby and Will.
The young actors who made these scripts happen.

CONTENTS

	Acknowledgments	i
1	Introduction	1
2	A Park	3
3	The Girl Who Cried Wolf	10
4	12 Angry People	19
5	Panto	24
6	Homeless	35
7	The Letter	44
8	Wall	48
9	Cell	54
10	Two Acting Exercises	66
11	Romeo and Juliet Extract	73

ACKNOWLEDGMENTS

I'd like to thank Sally for her proofreading skills, her collaboration and her patience. Also, the Brewery Arts Centre in Kendal for their support, and for giving me the opportunity to teach the brilliant young people who inspired this book.

SHORT PLAYS FOR YOUNG PEOPLE AGED 11-15

A selection of varied, modern scenes and exercises for KS3 & KS4 English and drama students.

These short scenes were designed to solve a problem – a problem that I think many English and drama teachers and workshop leaders will identify with: What scripts are available for young people? I don't mean young adults, students aged sixteen and above, who can deal with more mature subject matter and language – I mean that awkward age between eleven and fifteen, the age when classic fairy tales are too young, but NT connections are too old. In this age range, pupils are maturing at hugely different rates, and finding work that 'fits all' is a nigh on impossible task. Too often drama teachers are forced into allowing students to create their own work when they aren't experienced enough to do so. Children come from all sorts of different backgrounds, from different cultures and with different religious beliefs, so finding modern texts they'll enjoy that won't elicit letters of complaint is often a very fine balancing act. Some parents are unhappy with their children using 'bad' language, others with overt discussions of sex or religion, so the teacher is either forced to heavily redact a script, sometimes making it barely useable, or simply rely on Shakespeare or other classic plays. Of course, there is nothing wrong with the classics, but contemporary drama and the spoken word has an immense power for young people, it excites them, it makes them feel heard and it helps them discuss issues they may feel uncomfortable dealing with in their lives.

These ages are where many young people are finding themselves, sometimes struggling with identity and always being besieged on all sides by a cacophony of information that can be overwhelming. Often young people at these ages feel unheard and unrepresented. I hope they can find characters and events they identify with in these pages – opportunities for their voices, talents and humour to be championed.

There is a wide range of pieces here, from storytelling perhaps more suited to the lower end of the range, to more complicated issue plays that will probably be preferred by older groups. If you teach at a drama club or youth theatre group as I do (hence the development of these plays), then there are pieces here that appeal to the entire range too. Most of the scenes have non-gendered roles that should help you with casting, and some can act as stimulus for further devising (something that would greatly help GCSE drama teachers as most exam specifications include devised performance exams) and some are deliberately written as exercises to teach different acting methodologies.

I hope you find them useful, and that your students enjoy them as much as mine did!

CJ.

A Park

This scene for six actors was based on a play some of my students and I saw as part of the National Theatre's 'Connections' performed by some older pupils. My group loved it – they loved the characters, the situation (in the NT play a girl had retreated up a tree rather than handcuffing herself to some swings), and the piece as a whole sparked a lot of discussion in the group about the frustrations young people feel about not being heard, not being 'seen' and hiding in their phones and social media, not because they want to particularly, but because it's what everyone else does.

Although they were very keen to do the NT Connections piece, there was some language and themes not altogether appropriate for the ages of that particular group (11-15), so I decided to write my own version. All the roles are non-binary, and the scene also deals with themes of individuality, diversity and bullying, and will hopefully spark many discussions after your class has watched the performance.

With my group, it went down very well. One of my students, after a little rehearsal, exclaimed "Hey, this is like the piece we saw! Cool."

A Park (6 actors)

A park. Early evening. Warm and still. Lounge lights flickering on in the distance, one by one. Mum's and Dad's pretending to watch the news.

QUINN wanders through the park alone. They half-heartedly push the roundabout, try the see-saw but there's no-one on the other side. Considers the swings. Sits on a swing. Slowly, deliberately, QUINN takes a pair of handcuffs from a pocket and locks themselves to one of the chains. QUINN then takes a key from a pocket, puts it in their mouth and tries to swallow it. Gags.

Coughs the key back up.

Looks around. Furtively replaces the key in the pocket.

Beat.

JO enters, carrying a bag and a 'grabber'. They're litter picking. QUINN watches JO, who doesn't at first acknowledge them. JO bends down and picks something up.

JO: Absolutely disgusting. Who, in their right mind, brings a toilet brush to the park? What were they brushing? You don't see that every day. If I could get Hold of them, I'd shove this disgusting brush right up their-

At this point, JO realises they are not alone.

JO: Oh. Hello.

QUINN: Alright.

JO: It's not yours, is it?

QUINN: What?

JO: This!

JO brandishes the brush in a menacing way.

QUINN: Obviously not.

JO: Nothing's obvious in this game.

QUINN: What are you doing? I mean – why are you..?

JO: Someone's got to. Have you seen the state of this place?

Beat.

QUINN: Don't you go to St. Wilfred's?

JO: Yeah.

QUINN: I thought I'd seen you before somewhere…

JO: I've been in your history class for two years.

QUINN: Really?

JO: Yep.

ALEX AND SAM, out jogging, appear, racing each other to the see-saw. ALEX wins, just.

ALEX: Beat you!

SAM: I gave you a head start.

ALEX: Oh no, you're not doing this again…

SAM: Not doing what?

ALEX: Making up excuses, you're always making up-

SAM: Alright, alright – you win the sprint, but I definitely did more press-ups.

ALEX: By, like, half a rep.

SAM: A win is a win.

ALEX: So... what's the decider?

SAM: Who can go highest on the swings.

ALEX: What? That's not a proper sport.

SAM: Chicken.

ALEX: I can definitely swing higher.

SAM: Come on then!

The two run to the swings, but are suddenly aware of QUINN.

SAM: Hello.

QUINN: Hello.

ALEX: Could you er... vacate your swing for a minute please?

SAM: We've got a very important competition to finish.

QUINN: 'Fraid not.

QUINN holds up their hand, still cuffed to the swing.

ALEX: Who did that?

SAM: That's awful!

JO: They did it themselves.

QUINN: How d'you know that?

JO: Process of deduction. No injuries. No sign of a struggle. Pretty obvious.

Beat.

QUINN: I wondered if you'd noticed. Did it not occur to you to ask me why?

JO: Not really. Each to their own. I'm collecting toilet brushes.

ALEX: Why er... why did you, *how* did you?

QUINN: That's not important. That doesn't matter. What matters is I've swallowed the key and I'm not getting off.

SAM: Er... OK. Why did you..?

QUINN: Because it's all fake. Everything. No one ever talks about anything. Maybe if I do this people will take notice, people will listen.

ALEX: Listen to what?

QUINN: To each other! For a change. I go home, everyone just stares at their phones, at the telly. I do it, I'm just as bad! I want people to look straight at me – not just 'like' my pictures on a screen.

SAM: Blimey.

ALEX: OK. Er...

During this exchange, JO has retreated to the roundabout.

JO: That's pretty cool actually.

QUINN: Thanks.

BILLY and CHARLIE enter. Bored. Looking for entertainment. Notice JO on their own.

BILLY: What's in the bag, loser?

CHARLIE: Give us a look.

BILLY: Yeah, show us what you got. Is it food?

CHARLIE: We're starving.

BILLY: Starving.

CHARLIE: Yeah, Billy's always hungry.

Beat.

JO: It's mine.

BILLY: Wow! Bravery!

CHARLIE: Unusual.

BILLY: But stupid. Give it here.

CHARLIE: Now.

JO thinks for a second, then throws the bag to them.

JO: Take it then!

The contents deposit themselves on BILLY and CHARLIE.

BILLY: Hey!

CHARLIE: That's disgusting!

JO tries to make a run for it, BILLY catches him.

BILLY: Not so fast, tramp. You might wanna eat this, but we don't.

CHARLIE: It stinks. You stink. You've made Billy mad, haven't you? That's never a good idea. What you gonna do with this piece of rubbish, Bill?

BILLY: Gonna make them sorry, make them apologise, aren't we? Tell you what, why don't you chew on this?

BILLY reaches in the bag for something disgusting and tries to force it into JO's mouth while CHARLIE holds JO still. JO squirms. At the height of the struggle, they realise they're not alone.

SAM: I think you should leave it.

ALEX: Yeah. Leave it. Back off.

BILLY and CHARLIE drop JO (and the rubbish) and square up to SAM and ALEX.

BILLY: Why, what're you gonna do about it?

CHARLIE: Yeah, what're you gonna do?

ALEX: My mate's just done about a million press-ups, you wanna watch it!

SAM: And, more importantly, Billy Hogg, I'll tell your mum.

BILLY stops in his tracks.

BILLY: You... your mum does pilates with my mum. I've seen you.

SAM: That's right.

CHARLIE: Billy, smack him one!

BILLY: Listen er...

Beat.

BILLY: Hang on, why is that weirdo handcuffed to a swing?

JO: They're protesting.

BILLY: Nobody asked you.

CHARLIE: Yeah, nobody asked you, trash breath. Protesting what?

ALEX: About life. Nobody talks to each other, or something.

QUINN: Yeah, and in a weird sort of way, it seems to be working.

The Girl who Cried Wolf

This scene would be useful as a part of any English or drama scheme of work on stories with a message or a moral. From a drama perspective, it would also be useful when teaching students how to adapt traditional stories for performance, which is a direction some pupils enjoy taking in their devised work.

I produced this piece for performance, and it was very successful - there are some real opportunities for comedy and funny characterisation here, but I think in terms of the age range this collection is aimed at (11-15), I would suggest that of all the pieces, this is the one that sits most comfortably at the lower end of the range. Eleven, twelve and thirteen-year-olds will hopefully enjoy the modern retelling of the classic tale and will learn some simple staging and performance techniques.

I've deliberately written this for a shepherd GIRL, because I think girls often don't get the chance to play a central character in traditional stories who isn't a princess, but I think all the other parts can be played by any gender, the names of the villagers and the sheep can be changed to suit the pupil taking on the role.

THE GIRL WHO CRIED WOLF (7 - 9 Actors)

STORYTELLER 1: Once upon a time,

STORYTELLER 2: As these things so often are,

STORYTELLER 1: There lived a bored young shepherd girl,

STORYTELLER 2: Who didn't have a car.

Beat.

ST 1: What's that got to do with anything?

ST 2: Not much, but it rhymed, didn't it?

ST1: She lived on a quiet hill next to a mysterious wood where lurked many dangerous, wild animals.

ST 2: Working as a shepherd girl was a lonely occupation, and the girl was always bored.

ST 1: She wanted a distraction.

ST 2: But could never find satisfaction.

SHEPHERD GIRL: I am so bored. I haven't been this bored since mum and dad made me watch Bargain Hunt.

SHEEP 1 & 2: BAAA! BAAA! BAAA!

SHEEP 1: Don't be bored shepherd girl, there's LOADS to do!

SHEEP 2: You could eat grass?

SHEEP 1: You could run about a bit and go…

SHEEP 2: BAAAAAAAAA!

SHEEP 1: We could let a dog chase us?

SHEEP 2: We could follow each other about, like this!

SHEEP 1: Yes, like this!

SHEEP 2: Come and play!

SHEEP 1: Why don't you like hanging out with us?

SHEPHERD GIRL: I do, I'm just SO BORED. It's the same every day.

SHEEP 1: Well, if you're bored you could... well, you could-

SHEPHERD GIRL: What is it?

SHEEP 1: Pretend a wolf is attacking us, shout for help, we'll act all scared and stuff. I do an excellent dead sheep impression, LOOK!

SHEEP 2: What rubbish. You don't look dead, just stupid.

SHEPHERD GIRL: It's not rubbish, I think it's a great idea. Let's do it! WOLF! WOLF! HELP ME! THE BIG BAD WOLF IS AFTER MY LOVELY SHEEP!

ST1 and ST2 become VILLAGER 1 and VILLAGER 2, running to the stage holding sticks and waving them in the air. If you need a bigger cast, VILLAGER 1&2 can be separate characters.

VILLAGER 1 – Where did those nasty old wolves go?

VILLAGER 2 – I'll find them! I'll whack them and whack them and whack them!

VILLAGER 1 – Have they run away?

VILLAGER 2 – Are the sheep alright?

VILLAGER 1 – Look, there's a dead one there, oh no!

SHEEP 1 is doing his 'dead sheep' impression.

VILLAGER 2 – I don't think it LOOKS very dead. It keeps moving, see!

SG – Nothing to worry about, sorry, I made a mistake. I thought I saw wolves, but I must have been dreaming!

VILLAGER 1 – Oh ok, never mind, let's go back to the village.

The Townspeople become storytellers again, while the sheep and the shepherd girl all laugh.

SHEEP 2 – Teee heee heee! That was pretty funny...

SHEEP 1 – Did you see their faces?

SG – That was BRILLIANT.

ST 1 – Meanwhile, in the forest...

WOLF 1 – Hey, are you a wolf?

WOLF 2 – Yeah – you?

WOLF 1 – Yeah. Wanna hang out?

WOLF 2 – Definitely.

WOLF 1 – Got any food?

WOLF 2 – No, but... I have seen some real delicious looking sheep...

WOLF 1 – Really? Where?

WOLF 2 – Just on the other side of those trees. One of them was doing a REALLY bad impression of a dead sheep.

WOLF 1 – Wow. Maybe we should eat them.

WOLF 2 – I was thinking the same thing...

ST 2 – The very next day, the shepherd girl played the EXACT same trick again.

SG: WOLVES! WOLVES! THE BIG BAD WOLVES ARE COMING! HELP MEEEEEE!

VILLAGER 1 – Well done shepherd girl. Where did they go?

VILLAGER 2 – Did they go this way?

VILLAGER 1 – Or this way?

VILLAGER 2 – I'm gonna whack them and whack them and WHACK them!

VILLAGER 1 – I think you have some anger issues.

VILLAGER 2 – Let's GET THEM! We could follow their scent.

Villager 2 sniffs the air dramatically.

VILLAGER 1 – I can't smell a thing...

SG: Can you believe it? I'm so sorry, but I made a mistake AGAIN! I thought I saw wolves, but it must have been a mirage. They can happen sometimes you know, mirages.

VILLAGER 1 – I'm beginning to think,

VILLAGER 2 – You're playing a trick on us.

VILLAGER 1 – If you're not careful...

VILLAGER 2 – We'll have to whack you and whack you and WHACK you!

VILLAGER 1 – Come on Bob, let's get you home for a nice cup of tea.

TP become storytellers again.

SHEEP 2: Why didn't you tell us you were going to do it again?

SHEEP 1: We thought there was really a wolf!

SHEEP 2: You didn't let us in on the joke!

SG: Ha Ha! LOL! ROFL! You're all so silly.

SHEEP 1: You know what?

SHEEP 2: We're not gonna let you play with us now.

SHEEP 1: Nope. No chance. We're gonna follow each other about…

SHEEP 2: Do a bit of baaaaaing,

SHEEP 1: And YOU CAN'T PLAY. Come on Doris.

SHEEP 2: Coming Norman.

ST 1: The girl played the trick twice more…

ST 2: And the townsfolk kept being taken in.

ST 1: They weren't very bright to be honest.

ST 2: But one day…

WOLF 1: Look, over here!

WOLF 2: Over where?

WOLF 1: There! Two delicious looking sheep. Following each other round. Going baaa.

WOLF 2: Where?

WOLF 1: There!

WOLF 2: Where?

WOLF 1: Have you gone blind from wearing grandmama's glasses? There! Look OVER THERE!

WOLF 2: Oh yeah. There they are. Juicy.

WOLF 1: I can't wait for dinner tonight...

WOLF 2: Oooooh. What're you making?

WOLF 1: SHEEEEP! You idiot. Pay attention.

WOLF 2: Oh yeah. Come on then.

WOLF 1: Look, that shepherd girl is so bored she's not even watching her flock ... I'll get that one.

WOLF 2: OK. Which one shall I get?

WOLF 1: THAT ONE!

WOLF 2: Oh yeah, cool.

WOLVES prowl towards the sheep, unseen by the shepherd girl, indicating for the audience to be quiet.

WOLF 1: We're big bad wolves, so don't you bleat.

WOLF 2: We'll catch these sheep, turn 'em into meat.

WOLF 1 grabs SHEEP 2, WOLF 2 grabs SHEEP 1 and drags them USC.

SHEEP: BAAAAAAAA! BAAAAAAAAAA! BAAAAAAAA!

SHEPHERD GIRL: WOLF! There's a wolf! WOLF! Ahhh! There's another one! There's TWO wolves and they're attacking! They've got my sheep! HELP ME!

(SG sits down and cries with her hands over her eyes)

ST 1: But no one came...

ST 2: They didn't believe her anymore.

VILLAGER 1: Oh, listen to that, shouting away again.

VILLAGER 2: THAT GIRL! When I get hold of her, I'm gonna whack her and whack her and...

VILLAGER 1: I know, I know. Calm down. Bargain Hunt's just starting.

SHEEP 1: I can guess what you're thinking...

SHEEP 2: You're wondering what happened to us poor sheep.

SHEEP 1: Well fortunately for us, I always carry an emergency Greggs vegan sausage roll in my er... fleece, and I convinced those hungry wolves to eat that instead.

Sheep 1 produces a Greggs bag, Sheep 2 does the same, they hand them to the wolves, who smell them cautiously, then eat.

WOLF 1: Oh my! It's just like the real thing! I'm converted.

WOLF 2: It also has much less of a carbon footprint.

WOLF 1: Wow! Did it make you clever too? Come on, let's go and open a salad bar...

Wolves exit. Sheep play dead. SG looks up.

SG: OH NO! MY LOVELY SHEEP!

SHEEP 1: Don't fret.

SHEEP 2: We were just pretending.

SG: Phew! From now on I'll never tell lies and start amending!

EVERYONE: HURRAY!

ST 1: The moral of the story is...

ST 2: NEVER inflict Bargain Hunt on your children?

ST 1: NO! The moral is...

WHOLE CAST: If you want to be trusted, tell the truth!

12 Angry People

The title gives it away, right? Just like the classic play and film, this scene is about twelve people, locked in a room, trying to decide somebody's fate. There are two clear sides: jurors **1, 2, 6, 8, 9, 10, 11** are all in favour of a GUILTY verdict, whilst **3, 4, 5** and **12** are on the NOT GUILTY side. **7**, significantly, is undecided.

My groups found this an empowering experience, even as a performance, to imagine their opinions having so much importance that somebody's liberty depended on them. The scene raises several issues and discussion-starters about the law, identity, and the definition of guilt. There are also discussions to be had about prejudice, race and sexuality. I would recommend this scene for ages 12 and above, particularly because some of the vocabulary is quite advanced.

The scene acts well as a devising stimulus, coming from the angle of either asking the students to question and present 'what happens next?', but also as inspiration for their own 'courtroom' pieces.

12 Angry People (12 actors)

A room with a large table in the centre, surrounded by chairs. THE JURY sit around the table; they look as if they have been here for some time.

JUROR 1 (The Foreperson): Well. Here we are. Deadlocked at eight to four. Seven of us strongly believe the defendant to be guilty, four continue to vote not guilty and one of us, Juror 7, is still 'undecided'-

JUROR 2: You have to make a decision!

JUROR 7: What?

JUROR 2: We've been here for two days. We've all decided. We all have an opinion. You have to have an opinion.

JUROR 1: If you might control yourself...

JUROR 2: Sorry, it's just-

JUROR 1: We've all been here a long time.

JUROR 2: Sorry. I'm-

JUROR 7: That's alright. It's somebody's life, you know?

JUROR 8: They should've thought about that.

JUROR 9: Before they ruined somebody else's.

JUROR 1: Ladies and gentlemen-

JUROR 3: Please don't use that phrase.

JUROR 1: I beg your pardon?

JUROR 4: Or that one. It's offensive.

JUROR 1: What is? I beg your pardon?

JUROR 4: No. "Ladies and Gentlemen". What if we're neither?

JUROR 10: For god's sake.

JUROR 5: Or what if we identify as a man or woman, but still don't want to be labelled as a 'lady' or a 'gentleman'?

JUROR 1: I apologise. I am trying, as best I can, to alleviate some of the tension in this room. This is a very important decision and I want us to try and address the case objectively.

JUROR 11: That's difficult though, isn't it?

JUROR 12: Why?

JUROR 11: Because of what you believe in life.

JUROR 12: I don't understand.

JUROR 11: You do. You're trying to provoke me. It's about the sort of person you are. Those of you voting not guilty, you sympathise with her – sorry, them, because THEY'RE one of you.

JUROR 12: One of who?

JUROR 6: If all you're going to do is ask questions, then how can anyone have a proper conversation?

JUROR 3: I believe Juror 12 was merely trying to understand some of the reductive statements that have been thrown around this table over the last few hours.

JUROR 10: I don't understand-

JUROR 4: -That much is obvious.

JUROR 10: -What is reductive about using the correct grammar in a sentence. If SHE identified as a crisp packet, should we refer to her as cheese and onion? Or is that offensive to flame-grilled steak?

JUROR 12: Now who's being provocative?

JUROR 6: What are you, a therapist?

JUROR 1: Ladie... I mean, JURORS. Please. This is getting us nowhere. The judge has said she will accept a majority verdict. So, let's try and give her one. Then we can all go home.

JUROR 2: Amen to that.

JUROR 8: It's straightforward. The defendant committed a crime.

JUROR 9: Exactly. Her, or rather THEIR actions were against the law. Physical violence is against the law in this country – it's black and white, that's it.

JUROR 6: Well said.

JUROR 3: But that's exactly the problem, isn't it? The issue ISN'T black and white, but you're interpreting it like that-

JUROR 4: Which is shocking.

JUROR 11: What does that mean?

JUROR 4: What do you think? If you can be judgemental, why can't we? Are you saying if the defendant was a middle-class white heterosexual man, you'd be condemning them and completely ignoring the mitigating circumstances?

JUROR 11: That's a pointless comparison, if...

JUROR 5: Go on! You were going to say this would never have happened to a white man, right?

JUROR 8: Well...

JUROR 12: And that's exactly the problem! It wouldn't have. It is incomparable, because this imaginary person wouldn't have been insulted like that in the first place.

JUROR 2: We all face difficult situations, every day, difficult people, abusive people. Sometimes you have to grin and bear it. We all understand-

JUROR 3: Do we? Every day? Every waking moment do we live fearful of what we are, who we are? Are we scared to walk down the street alone? Have we put up with this for all of our lives, grown up in a minority culture and always felt like we are something 'other'?

JUROR 5: Most of us haven't. We have no idea what it's like, none at all.

Pause.

JUROR 7: Not guilty.

JUROR 9: What?

JUROR 8: You're kidding.

JUROR 7: Not guilty.

Panto

I'm personally not a massive fan of the genre, but I've performed in several and there's no doubt about its popularity amongst young people and for many, it is their first experience of live performance; as such, its value cannot be underestimated. I recently staged a short piece with my 11–15-year-olds that explored different genres of theatre, and by far the section in which the parts were most coveted was this, the pantomime scene. They are stock characters that the pupils have watched on stage and screen for years – they understand them – they know what is required from their portrayal. Children understand the characters, their basic motivations and therefore scenes like this are an excellent way of helping young actors develop and grow in confidence.

There is plenty of audience interaction and a traditional 'ghost gag' that may need explaining. Breaking the fourth wall might not be something they're used to, and the audience will need encouragement at first to join in!

Panto (5-7 actors)

PARKER: When I grow up, I want to be on the stage. I dream of being a performer.

ABAZ: You are! You made it!

PARKER: No, that's not what I-

ABAZ: Look! The thing you're standing on. It's a stage. Mission accomplished.

PARKER: I mean for a career, but... Hang on, mum, dad, what are you doing here? So embarrassing.

Out of nowhere, PARKER's mum and dad enter.

PARKER'S DAD: You CAN'T be on stage for a career.

PARKER'S MUM: Totally preposterous! Be an accountant, like your father.

PARKER: I don't WANT to be an accountant! I can't add! Also, I don't care!

Again, out of nowhere, EZRA appears.

EZRA: Fear not! Help is at hand...

PARKER: Who are you?

EZRA: I'm your fairy godmother of course! Wow. I thought you wanted to be on the stage. Come with me... and you'll be ... in a world of pure imagination, take a look, and you'll see what you wanted...

ABAZ: Wow. Retro.

PARKER'S DAD: Can we come too?

EZRA: I think you'd better, all of you. We need a cast!

Short movement sequence where we go into panto land. ABAZ as the villain, PARKER'S PARENTS become MINIONS...

ABAZ: *(Evil laugh)* My minions, gather around.

MINION 1: Yes, oh evil one.

MINION 2: What dastardly deeds have you got planned?

ABAZ: I have heard there is a young "hero" who's trying to express themselves on stage. We must quash their dreams – such ideas are dangerous – find them and bring them to me.

MINION 2: Of course, your smelliness...

MINION 2 starts to leave. MINION 1 staring at ABAZ.

MINION 2: Well, come on!

MINION 1: Sorry, can't stop staring. He's just so eeeyvvvviiilll.

MINION 2 and MINION 1 exit.

ABAZ: They'll never be on the stage. I'll make sure of that.

ABAZ lets forth an evil laugh and exits, dramatically.

PARKER enters, alone and sad.

PARKER: Oh no! I can't find my fairy godmother ANYWHERE! They've brought me to this terrifying land and now they've flown off somewhere. Something about Peter Pan running out of fairy dust...

Enter BUTTONS (Can be played by MINION 1/PARKER's dad)

BUTTONS: Never fear Parker, I'll save you!

PARKER: Who on earth are you?

BUTTONS: I'm Buttons, of course! Your trusty sidekick. Look at my lovely shiny buttons, aren't they great? Shall we count them? Look, I've got one... two...

PARKER: Er...

BUTTONS: SORRY! Sorry. Was I counting my buttons again?

PARKER: Yes.

BUTTONS: I'm ALWAYS doing that. Mum keeps telling me to stop but– Oh look, here she comes now!

Enter DAME DORIS, skipping happily and waving to the audience.

BUTTONS: *(Sings)* Isn't she lovely, isn't she wonderful..?

DAME DORIS: Oh thank you, thank you! *(To audience)* Hello boys and girls! I said HELLO boys and girls! That's better. Now, I'm Dame Doris and Buttons here is my child. My lovely, lovely child.

BUTTONS is counting their buttons again.

DAME DORIS: They're not very bright to be honest, but they've got a good heart. *(To PARKER)* And who might you be?

PARKER: I'm PARKER.

DAME DORIS: OH WOW!

PARKER: What?

DAME DORIS: You're a HERO aren't you? I've seen your type before. Every panto, every fairy tale, they've all got one you know, sometimes a prince, sometimes a princess, sometimes Sleeping Beauty, sometimes Cinderella, sometimes Dick–

PARKER and BUTTONS make shocked noises – this needs to be timed well.

DAME DORIS: -Whittington! What? What did you think I was going to say? Honestly. Young people nowadays.

BUTTONS: So... why did you look all sad just before we arrived?

PARKER: Well, there's a really evil villain trying to stop me fulfilling my dreams-

DAME DORIS: NO!

BUTTONS: That's awful! Everyone should be allowed all the cream they want!

Beat.

DAME DORIS: What?

BUTTONS: You said they aren't allowed cream! That's awful. I love cream. You can have it in cakes, in chocolate eclairs, in biscuits, in pasta sauce if you're swanky, on toast if you're ambitious...

They trail off mid-sentence.

DAME DORIS: What ARE you talking about, you stupid child! Parker here said they're not being allowed to fulfil their DREAMS, not CREAMS. It's that evil Abaz up to their old tricks again.

BUTTONS: OH. Right, yeah, that does make more sense. Well, I suppose we'd better find that evil old villain and teach them a lesson!

DAME DORIS: Yes. If only we knew where to find their lair...

BUTTONS: I know where to find their hair. It'll be on their head!

DAME DORIS: Their LAIR! You ridiculous person... Unless of course ABAZ is wandering about somewhere... but where could they be?

All three face the audience in a line.

BUTTONS: Hm. Tricky.

YOUNG ACTORS

DAME DORIS: Hmmmm.

PARKER: Hmmmmm.

ABAZ appears up stage, crossing from left to right and making 'shushing' mimes.

BUTTONS: *(To the audience)* What was it? What? WHAT? It was Abaz the evil? And WHERE were they? BEHIND US? Oh no they weren't... etc. Well I'm sorry, I REFUSE to believe Abaz would be here, now.

DAME DORIS: Totally preposterous.

BUTTONS: But just in case you DO see Abaz again, make sure you shout as loudly as you can, will you do that? Thanks. I'm really scared though.

PARKER: It's alright Buttons, you'll be ok.

DAME DORIS: Sometimes, when I'm afraid, I sing a little song and that makes me feel a bit braver.

BUTTONS: Ok, great idea, let's all sing 'If you're happy and you know it'. *(To audience)* But don't forget you lot, if you see Abaz the evil, shout as loudly as you can!

They all sing. ABAZ crosses back across the stage. Audience shouts. BUTTONS stops them singing. ABAZ returns to the stage and dances about behind them.

BUTTONS: Who was it? *(Response)* ABAZ? Oh no! And WHERE are they? Behind us? Alright, alright, we'll take a look.

All three do a comedy look behind, ABAZ ducks, they all turn back to audience.

BUTTONS: There was nothing there! Oh no there wasn't etc. Look, are you sure Abaz the evil is behind us? Ok, we'll take a look THIS WAY.

BUTTONS leads the three of them round in a circle 'looking' for ABAZ. ABAZ joins the back of the line, then when the three of them return to their line facing the audience, ABAZ exits.

BUTTONS: There was NOTHING there! Oh no there wasn't! etc.

DAME DORIS: Boys and girls, boys and girls, WHO was it you saw? ABAZ the evil? Well, we'll have to sing it AGAIN then won't we wooo!

They all sing the song again. ABAZ appears behind them. Audience shout. ABAZ taps BUTTONS on the shoulder who screams and runs away. ABAZ follows. Mid song, the dame realizes what's happened and screams.

PARKER: What is it?

DAME DORIS: My darling Buttons! Gone! Who could have done such a thing?

PARKER: *(To the audience)* Did you lot see who took Buttons? Oh my goodness! Abaz the evil?

DAME DORIS: Well if Abaz the evil was here, why didn't you tell us? *(Audience response – hopefully pretty loud and frustrated by now)* Well you'll have to be much louder than that next time won't you and well, we'll, have to sing it again then won't we wooooo!

Sequence repeats, but this time with PARKER running off. The Dame is left alone on stage singing, screams when she realizes PARKER has gone.

DAME DORIS: Oh my goodness who's taken Parker? *(audience response)* Oh NO! Well why didn't you say so? Well you'll have to be much louder next time won't you and well, I'll have to sing it again they won't I woooo!

DAME DORIS sings again, the sequence repeats, but this time ABAZ takes Doris' hand and starts dancing with her.

Slowly, realisation dawns and Doris stops dancing and singing.

DAME DORIS: Wait… everyone has gone, so I must be dancing with… who is it? *(audience response)* Oh. Alright. I've got this. I'm going to take a look in 1, 2, 3!

Doris looks at ABAZ, who screams and runs off stage.

DAME DORIS: Well, CHARMING!

DAME DORIS exits on the opposite side of the stage to ABAZ.

PARKER enters.

PARKER: Well, that got me a long way. I'm still no nearer to realising my dreams and now I'm all alone again. *(PARKER looks very sadly at the audience and waits for an 'ahhhhhhh')* A bit more than that, come on! *(Hopefully a louder 'ahhhhhhhhh')* That's more like it.

ABAZ dashes on stage, as if still running from the dame, sees PARKER and tries to 'style it out', as if they weren't running away at all.

ABAZ: What? I wasn't running away! Nope.

PARKER: I didn't say anything…

ABAZ: No matter. *(ABAZ checks behind to make sure the dame isn't there, evil laugh)* You're coming with me, back to my lair!

ABAZ laughs manically and drags PARKER to their evil lair.

PARKER: Are we here already? That was quick.

ABAZ: Oh yeah, it was only up the road. I mean, QUIET MORTAL!

EZRA enters, brandishing their wand.

EZRA: Not so fast, ugly!

ABAZ: Ah! How dare you! I was voted best looking villain on Instavillain three years running... How did you get in here?

EZRA: It wasn't that hard. Your followers are pretty stupid. I told them we were playing hide and seek and that they had to count to 10,000. I think they're still going.

ABAZ: Not surprising. They only know as far as 7.

PARKER: Thank goodness you're back fairy godmother, I've had the weirdest time...

EZRA: Yeah, sorry about that. Had to sort out an awful mess, he fell right out of the sky. Talk about going to Never Never Land.

ABAZ: SILENCE! I will destroy your dreams right here and now!

EZRA: Not so fast dung breath!

PARKER: You can't destroy my dreams, they're too strong!

ABAZ: Ugh! I think I'm gonna be sick...

MINION 1 rushes in.

MINION 1: We've found her oh dark one – look she's right there!

ABAZ: I know, dingbat.

MINION 2 runs in.

MINION 2: EIGHT! EIGHT comes after seven!

MINION 1: SHUSH! She tricked us... You're making us look like idiots.

EZRA: You're doing a pretty good job of that yourself.

ABAZ: QUIET FOOLS! Your time has come, I've had enough of this, when I've finished with you, you will NEVER BE ON STAGE AGAIN!

PARKER: I'm not afraid of you.

ABAZ is stopped in his tracks. MINION 2 and MINION 1 shocked. EZRA smiles in triumph.

PARKER: I'll be what I want, do what I want.

MINION 1: You go girl!

Everyone looks at MINION 1.

MINION 1: Sorry, carry on.

As PARKER talks, ABAZ and MINIONs react as if they are being slowly destroyed.

PARKER: Panto was the first time I ever went to the theatre, and I was mesmerised. You can do anything on a stage, and that's where I'm meant to be. I don't have to do what you tell me.

EZRA: Finish them off!

ABAZ and the MINIONs are on their knees.

ABAZ: No, wait...

PARKER: You have no power over me!

ABAZ, MINION 2 and MINION 1 are destroyed, all three in a heap.

EZRA: You did it!

PARKER: Thanks for your help.

EZRA: Just doing my job – now I must be off, someone in Carlisle *(Or local town)* just said they don't believe in fairies, so I'm gonna have a word.

PARKER: Farewell fairy godmother, I'll never forget you!

EZRA exits.

PARKER: And they all lived... *(PARKER looks down at the heap of 'baddies')* Well, most of them, lived HAPPILY EVER AFTER... THE END!

PARKER bows, looks down at the 'bodies', shrugs and exits.

Homeless

This scene is probably my favourite of the collection. It raises the issue of people forced to live on the streets, but at the same time, it gives the 'Stranger Things' and the roleplay fans a chance to take on some classic characters through the vehicle of the young people trying to provide themselves with some entertainment and escapism in their desperate situation. They fulfil these archetypes within the group, whilst also delivering monologues to an imaginary camera, allowing students to experience delivering speeches to an audience.

The character names are intentionally genderless and it's interesting to observe the role each student gravitates towards and why. There are sections where 'time passes' – a deliberately vague stage direction that invites the pupils to devise different ways of representing this. The other challenge of the scene is to decide where the 'invisible' passersby are. One group I taught used the audience, which was particularly effective at drawing them into the action. I would recommend this as a script only attempted later in a course, after the pupils have had some experience of different staging methodologies, then they will be more able to devise their own material. It could even be used as the basis for an assessed GCSE scripted piece.

Homeless (6 actors)

A town. Under a bridge. Early evening. People leaving work, bustling, drinking with friends. WIZARD, BITEY, SOLDIER and LEADER are huddled under blankets and coats, curled up against the Autumn chill. A cap sits in front of them, a few twenty pence pieces and one fifty at the bottom.

WIZARD: Spare some change please? We haven't eaten for two days.

SOLDIER: A bit of change? Not eaten since yesterday morning.

Beat.

WIZARD: Two days sounds better.

SOLDIER: Sorry?

WIZARD: Two days sounds better than yesterday morning.

SOLDIER: What difference does it make?

WIZARD: Life or death mate. Difference between getting 50p or someone nipping into the Sainsbury's mini-mart and getting us a full-on meal deal. Ham and smoked cheese, beef hoola-hoops and a rockstar.

Beat. They consider this.

LEADER: Sainsbury's Local.

WIZARD: Same difference.

LEADER: Mini mart? Where d'you think we are? Downtown Hollywood?

WIZARD: If only.

SOLDIER: Why? For that one time Steven Spielberg is walking by, sees through all the grime to your perfect, flawless face and knows in that one moment that he needs you, and only you, to play the lead in his next mega blockbuster and immediately advances you a briefcase full of fourteen million dollars, half now, half when the film's in the can?

Beat.

WIZARD: Yep. That's about right.

BITEY emerges from what had appeared to be only a pile of coats, holding an imaginary camera.

BITEY: Lights, camera, ACTION! Zooming in for your close-up, really close, ooops, not that close, can see right up your nose... headshot. Ready for your monologue? Aaand.... ACTION.

WIZARD: I've finally done it. The beast lies dead at my feet and the village is safe. It has taken most of my magic, so much of my energy, my time, eaten into my life like the jaws of evil itself, gnawing at the shreds of my soul, but somehow... somehow I found the courage, the power, I drew from the great wisdom of my kind and now I shall return to from whence I came... never to be seen again.

SOLDIER and BITEY applaud.

BITEY: Panning left, long-shot.

BITEY pans the camera onto SOLDIER

SOLDIER: Darling I've got to go. My country needs me. I can't just stand by while the world falls apart. It is my duty, my sacred calling. This is what all the years of training have been for – preparing me for this moment. No... don't cry, don't. I'll be back before you know it and then the world will be free. Tell little Janey I love her. Goodbye.

More applause.

BITEY: Now to our great and fearless commander...

BITEY focuses the camera onto LEADER

LEADER: Don't be stupid. I'm not in the mood for messing about.

Beat.

BITEY: Is that it? That wasn't very good.

LEADER: I mean it. You need to be preserving energy, keeping warm – while you've been mucking about a hundred people have walked past, unaware we're even here, about to spend £3.50 on a vanilla chai latte with cream, soya milk and a sprinkle of chocolate shaved from the paw of a meerkat – wasting their money - when they could feed two of us for that price. If you're gonna survive, you've gotta get your heads in the game.

Beat. Everyone breaks into applause.

LEADER: Idiots.

SCOUT and MONK appear, carrying a bag.

SCOUT: What's going on stinkers?

BITEY: No noise on set!

SCOUT: Films? Excellent. My scene?

BITEY aims the camera at SCOUT.

BITEY: Aaaand, ACTION!

SCOUT: I have returned. The mission was hard, but I think I found a way through. I spent the entire night disguised as an otter, sniffing about on the riverbank – the enemy suspected nothing. My otter noise *(demonstrates)* was far too convincing. If you can find the courage to come with me, we can follow the river, through the mountains and there we will find horses waiting that can take us back to safety. You must all be brave, swift and silent as the night. Come, friends!

Applause.

LEADER: What did you get?

SCOUT: Nothing.

MONK: Well, next to nothing. It was hopeless really. Found a couple of half-eaten burgers but they looked like they'd been there all week.

SCOUT: Sort of soggy.

MONK: And a bit green. Don't want a repeat of the fish fingers incident.

SCOUT: Nasty.

SCOUT and BITEY mime vomiting.

MONK: Exactly. We went to Pret as well, but everything had gone, those lot from the park must have gotten up so early – the guy gave us a muffin but er... well...

SCOUT: It was only small.

LEADER: So what was the point in sending you out!

MONK: Sorry?

LEADER: If you were just gonna go off on a jolly – wandering about in the park eating muffins while we're all grafting away here for...

(LEADER checks the hat) seventy-three pence and what looks like a Hatchimal.

MONK: Calm down. We weren't on a 'jolly' and we shared ONE muffin. Singular. And it was stale.

LEADER: Oh bless you! I'm so sorry you had to eat a stale muffin! Why does it always feel like I'm the only one doing anything around here!

BITEY: I'm hungry.

PAUSE. Time passes.

The same place. Later that night. Everyone huddles together for warmth. SOLDIER sits cross-legged by the change hat. BITEY stirs.

BITEY: Lights, camera...

MONK: Not now Bitey. Later.

BITEY: I'm sitting at the head of a huge table. There's just me. The whole thing is covered in roast beef, roast ham, burgers, chips, Yorkshire pudding and gravy. Not a vegetable in sight, vegetables illegal in my kingdom, but at least seventeen pints of gravy...

SCOUT: Oddly specific.

BITEY: ...A whole cow, piles of potatoes... and just me and my knife and fork.

SOLDIER: Go back to sleep. Spare some change mate? No..? You've just got your card? No worries. Thanks anyway.

Beat.

SOLDIER: Any change please? Sorry. No, I'm not looking for trouble.

Sorry. If I had a home, I'd go there. Cheers.

PAUSE. *Time passes.*

The same place. The next morning. Cold. Everyone is awake, but quiet. All sitting except BITEY, who is still curled up, shivering.

LEADER: Thanks very much. Means a lot.

WIZARD: Was that a fiver?

LEADER: Yeah. Reckon we can get down the shops soon.

WIZARD: Sandwiches AND cups of tea?

LEADER: Maybe. Depends what's on special.

MONK: Any change please?

SOLDIER: Any change?

SCOUT: Some change please? Woah! Sorry. I didn't mean... hey, calm down!

SCOUT and SOLDIER on their feet.

SOLDIER: There's no need for that!

SCOUT: Hey! That hurt! Get out of it!

WIZARD: Yeah, get lost!

EVERYONE on their feet now except BITEY.

LEADER: Leave us alone. Now. We're not doing any harm.

SOLDIER: Hey. Put that away.

LEADER: Someone might get hurt.

MONK: Alright. Alright. Take it.

MONK hands over the hat.

SCOUT: Don't! We've worked all day for that!

LEADER: It's not worth it. Let it go. Better hungry than hurt.

PAUSE. Time passes.

The next night. All sitting back in a line. BITEY still shivering under a blanket.

LEADER: Spare some change?

SCOUT: Any change please?

WIZARD: Are we invisible? Bit of CHANGE PLEASE? Sorry.

SOLDIER: Any food?

MONK: Anything at all?

Beat. BITEY coughs.

WIZARD: Are they ok d'you think?

SCOUT: Dunno.

LEADER: We need to get them something. Maybe take them to a shelter.

WIZARD: They told us to go home last time, remember?

Beat.

BITEY: Lights...

LEADER: Not now.

BITEY: Camera…

LEADER: Too tired. Spare some change please?

BITEY: Action. Please?

MONK: My dear brothers, sisters and those who do not wish to be labelled as either – hear my sermon and hear it well. Please understand. We're not here to upset or offend you. We're not here on purpose. We're not invisible. We're closer than you think. Life is complicated, and sometimes it's difficult. It's much easier for some people and that doesn't really seem fair. We're not asking for much, just that you notice us. If you allow yourself to look, you'll find that you can help – it's easy – we don't want to rob you, or hurt you. We don't want to threaten your way of life. If you live with your eyes closed it's no life at all. Open your eyes. Amen.

BITEY: Aaaand… Cut.

The Letter

This scene is deliberately open-ended, because it is intended to act as a devising stimulus and is also useful as an extension to a traditional Stanislavsky 'What If?' imagination workshop.

Students will be encouraged to manipulate the audiences' focus and create tension through their performance, then will decide what is in the envelope and how they will react in the moment to portray this coherently to their audience.

Roles are not gendered, as usual.

The Letter (5 Actors)

A group of people standing round a table. On the table is a sealed envelope.

ARDEN: What's in it, d'you think?

ZANE: Who sent it?

ARDEN: Don't know. It's completely blank.

Pause.

SACHA: Should we open it?

MURPHY: I guess that's what whoever sent it wants us to do.

ELLIS: We should be careful. It might be a trap?

ZANE: How can it be a trap?

ELLIS: Haven't you ever heard of letter-bombs?

ZANE: It isn't big enough, surely...

ELLIS: It's a figure of speech. Could be a deadly chemical.

ARDEN: Chemical warfare.

SACHA: You never know, these days.

Pause.

MURPHY: Should we destroy it then?

ARDEN: How?

MURPHY: Burn it?

ELLIS: That might set it off. Whatever it is.

ZANE: Yeah. You've got a point there.

SACHA: A good point that one.

ARDEN: Yeah. Good point.

Pause.

ELLIS: Perhaps we should take a closer look.

ZANE: An inspection?

ELLIS: Yeah, an inspection. Check it out in more detail.

ARDEN: Ok. Let's look. But. Slowly does it.

As one, the group edges towards the table. Considers the envelope more closely.

MURPHY: White.

SACHA: Plain.

ZANE: Not a mark on it.

ELLIS: No writing, nothing.

Pause.

ARDEN: That's weird, isn't it?

MURPHY: Yeah. Weird.

ZANE reaches out to the letter.

ELLIS: DON'T!

ZANE picks it up, turns it over, lays it face down.

ZANE: Blank on the other side too.

SACHA: Sealed tight.

ELLIS: Something inside though.

MURPHY: Definitely something inside.

ARDEN: A clear lump.

ZANE: A lump?

SACHA: Small lump. Maybe paper, but you can see there's-

MURPHY: -something else. A darker colour. Small.

Pause.

ELLIS: Think we ought to..?

MURPHY: Yeah. I think it's time.

ARDEN: Ok, here goes...

Wall

This piece is the only in the collection with female identifying roles. It was written for a group I taught that was dominated by students identifying as female, and they wanted me to write them a piece which, in their words, reflected "what it's like living in this boring place!"

The scene has elements of humour, whilst also inspiring discussions about peer pressure, individuality and asking questions about why people behave in the way that they do. It can also act as an effective devising stimulus because there is scope to ask the students to explore and portray what happens next.

Wall (3 Actors)

A sleepy town on a hot day. Nothing ever happens here. The air is thick and the tarmac bubbles. JESS, LACEY and ANNA are sitting on a wall, staring at nothing.

JESS: Hear that?

LACEY: What?

JESS: Long-tailed tit.

Beat.

LACEY: What?

JESS: Long-tailed tit. That sound.

LACEY: What?

JESS: Listen!

Silence. Listening.

JESS: There! D'you hear it?

ANNA: I can only hear birds.

JESS: Exactly! Long-tailed tit!

ANNA: What did you call me?

JESS: Nothing. You're hopeless.

Silence.

JESS: Wanna go to the park?

LACEY: What for?

JESS: Better than here.

LACEY: Stinks.

ANNA: And there'll be those idiots. They're always there. Remember the last time?

LACEY: They get all excited when girls turn up.

ANNA: Start showing off.

LACEY: What is it about riding a scooter down a slide they think we'll find impressive?

ANNA: Not sure.

JESS: It is weird.

Beat.

ANNA: So...

LACEY: So...

JESS: What about a game of truth or dare?

ANNA: A game?

JESS: Yeah, they don't bite.

ANNA: Funny.

LACEY: I dare you both to shut up.

ANNA: Alright then. My go. I dare you to go down the shops and steal something.

Beat.

JESS: Don't be-

LACEY: Haha, yeah. Gotta be more than a tenner though.

ANNA: Exactly. Not getting away with a Kitkat chunky.

JESS: I don't want to.

ANNA: Baby. It's your game. You suggested it, remember?

LACEY: True. It was your idea Jess, after all.

JESS: I-

ANNA: Do it.

LACEY: DO IT!

LACEY & ANNA: *(chanting)* Do it, do it, do it, do it, do IT!

JESS: NO.

Beat.

ANNA: Suit yourself.

LACEY: Boring.

Long pause.

JESS: Can it be anything, as long as it's more than a tenner?

ANNA: I can't believe it!

LACEY: She's gonna do it!

ANNA: Amazing! Yeah, anything.

LACEY: Then bring it back here.

ANNA: We'll wait for you.

Beat.

ANNA: Go on then.

JESS: You'll be here?

LACEY: Right here.

JESS: Hear that?

ANNA: What?

JESS: Woodpecker.

Beat.

JESS: Alright. I'm going.

JESS exits. LACEY watches her go.

LACEY: D'you think she'll do it?

ANNA: Nah. Maybe. Who cares? Funny though.

LACEY: Hope she doesn't get caught.

ANNA: She won't.

LACEY: No, but if she does…

ANNA: She won't.

LACEY: She's not like everyone else.

Beat.

LACEY: All the stuff with the birds. She's interested in stuff. She doesn't belong here.

Beat.

LACEY: We shouldn't have–

ANNA: For god's sake Lace! If you're so worried about her, you do it! It's only a laugh. Nothing ever happens – it's just a laugh, stop being boring.

Beat.

LACEY: I'm gonna stop her. Don't care what you think.

LACEY exits.

ANNA: Loser. Go on then, run after her.

Beat.

ANNA: She's not different. We're all the same.

Beat. Birdsong. ANNA finds a stone and flings it.

ANNA: Stupid birds – shut up! SHUT UP! SHUT UP!

Cell

Welcome to the longest scene of the collection. This is probably the most complex of all the scenes and would make an excellent basis for a GCSE scripted piece, or inspiration for devised work. Having said that, some of my younger students reacted very well to it – there are things here that lots of pupils have seen in TV dramas.

There are choices to be made here about where they are – is it a purely naturalistic cell in a prison or are the characters hostages, is there a deeper symbolic meaning? The suggestions made by my group ranged from purgatory, to dreams and nightmares, to (believe it or not) a "metaphor for life"! This will hopefully encourage the imaginations of your students to run wild – they need to decide how to stage the piece based on what they decide it means. What do they want their audience to take from the scene? It's a good script to use when you're helping pupils to understand the power of drama to convey messages and make people consider their lives, consider how they treat others and interact with them. Each character here is incarcerated, but each character reacts very differently to their incarceration. One of my favourite questions to ask after watching groups perform this is, "why does JO stay behind?"

Parts are not gendered, as usual.

Cell (5 Actors)

A cell. Two crates for sitting. One window, high in the wall USC. The door is in the 'invisible' wall DSC.

JO sits alone, staring into space, their eyes glazed.

JO: You are my sunshine, my only sunshine. You make me happy when skies are grey. You'll never know dear, how much I love you. Oh please don't take my sunshine away.

Beat.

A jangling of keys, a shutter is opened.

GUARD: Back against the wall, you know the drill.

JO stands facing the back wall, hands clearly visible. Shutter closes, door opens. LEE and VIV are thrown / pushed into the cell one at a time. LEE lands in a heap and weeps. VIV struggles but is pushed to the floor.

GUARD: I can chain you to the ceiling if that's what you want? Chain you by the ankles and leave you hanging. Is that what you want?

VIV glares at the GUARD.

GUARD: No good looking at me like that. Only doing my job. You should count yourself lucky you're in here. There's worse places to be. And... it'll be over soon. *(Indicating LEE)* Can you do something about that?

LEE's sobs grow louder. VIV glares.

GUARD: Oi! Shut up, can you?

GUARD: Will you shut up?!

Beat.

GUARD walks over to LEE, grabs them by the hair.

GUARD: Will you SHUT UP!

LEE wails louder.

GUARD: SHUT UP!

GUARD throws LEE to the ground, aims a kick. LEE is silent and still. VIV stands up.

JO: Don't.

GUARD and VIV turn to JO, as if noticing them for the first time.

GUARD: It's good advice. That one. They'll tell you how it is here. When I come, you get back against the wall, hands up. You don't interfere. Never interfere. OK?

Beat.

GUARD: Good.

GUARD exits, slamming the door and locking it behind them.

Beat.

JO approaches LEE, helps them to their feet and sits them on a crate.

JO: You ok?

Beat. LEE looks at JO.

JO: I know it's all a bit much right now. I was like that at first. The guard's right. There are worse places than this you know. Much worse.

Beat.

JO: I'm not saying you should be grateful or anything. Nothing like that. But, you've got to make the best of it, haven't you? Do what you can.

VIV: If you say look on the bright side, I'm gonna swing for you.

JO: I'm Jo.

VIV: I don't care, Jo.

LEE: Hi Jo.

JO: Hi.

LEE: I'm Lee.

JO: Nice to meet you, Lee.

LEE: Thanks.

VIV: Wow. I'm welling up. How are we going to get out?

VIV starts circling the cell, looking for escape. Tries the door. Pushes LEE off the crate, piles the crates on top of each other and tries to see out of the window, USC.

JO: Don't. Don't look.

Beat. VIV is clearly affected by what they have seen. Slowly climbs down.

LEE: What is it?

VIV: Light. There's so much light. So bright. Couldn't really make it out. Don't think. Don't think there's a way out.

Beat. JO approaches the crates, sets them apart, away from the window. Indicates for LEE and VIV to sit. Slowly, they do so.

JO: So... you ok? They'll bring us food soon.

LEE: Good. Hungry.

VIV: Is it any good?

JO: No. Awful. But what d'you expect?

Beat.

JO: So-

VIV: Don't be asking me why I'm here.

Beat.

JO: What d'you expect?

VIV: I don't want to talk about it. I never thought I'd end up here. Didn't think... Never imagined.

JO: None of us do.

LEE: I hurt someone.

Pause.

VIV: You?

LEE: I think that's why I'm here. I didn't mean to, I was standing up for what I believe in *(LEE looks up to the ceiling, as if worried they're being listened to)*, I mean, believed in. I don't believe it anymore.

Footsteps. Jangling of keys. A shutter opens.

GUARD: Back against the wall. You know the drill.

JO indicates for the others to stand facing the wall.

JO: Hands out. Like this.

JO demonstrates. LEE and VIV copy. The door opens.

GUARD: IN! Get inside! And be grateful. You've been good - this is your reward.

GUARD pushes in CAL who is either blindfolded or has a bag over their head. Hands tied together. CAL falls to their knees, breathing heavily.

CAL: Thank you.

GUARD: That's right. *(Speaking to the others, particularly VIV, who glares)* Respect, see?

GUARD exits. The door is shut. Keys rattle in the lock.

Beat.

CAL: Hello?

Beat.

CAL: Is anybody there?

The others approach slowly, cautiously. They inspect CAL. The following lines are whispered. CAL's head follows the sound.

LEE: Who is it?

JO: I've never seen them before.

VIV: It's probably a test. They're probably watching us, right now.

All three look up to the ceiling, then out to the door.

LEE: What should we do?

JO: We should probably help them.

VIV: What if they've been sent here to kill us? They might be armed.

LEE: They don't look armed.

JO: How can you tell?

LEE: I can tell. Nowhere for it to go.

VIV: Could be anywhere.

Beat.

CAL: Can er... can someone let me out please? My wrists hurt.

Beat.

LEE: What should we do?

JO: Not sure.

VIV: Gag them. Push them into the corner. Watch what they do.

LEE: No, there must be a better-

VIV: Kill them if we have to.

CAL: What did you say? I promise I'm not going to hurt anyone. I've been below, for months, but I kept quiet, did as I was told and they promised, they promised if I did as I was told they'd move me to a cell with a window. They promised.

Beat.

LEE: For goodness sake...

LEE goes to help CAL.

VIV: Don't!

LEE pulls off the blindfold.

Beat.

CAL: Hello.

JO: Hi.

LEE: Hello. You ok?

CAL: Sure. Better than I was, thanks. Can you..? *(CAL indicates their bound wrists)*

LEE: Of course.

JO: Are you sure?

VIV: Don't!

VIV approaches LEE. LEE puts up a hand.

LEE: I'll do what I want. I've been listening to you for too long.

VIV: You're putting us all in danger!

LEE: *(To CAL)* You're not going to hurt anyone, are you?

CAL: Course not.

LEE unties CAL's hands. VIV backs away. CAL stands.

CAL: See? Nothing to worry about.

CAL approaches VIV.

CAL: No weapons here.

CAL goes to pull out their pockets to show VIV.

VIV: GUARD! GUARD!

CAL: What is it? I'm not going to do anything.

JO: I think it's alright you know.

CAL approaches VIV, tries to put a consoling hand on their shoulder. VIV catches CAL's wrist and forces them down to the floor.

CAL: It's OK. Please don't get me sent back...

VIV: GUARD! GUARD!

Footsteps. Keys. A shutter.

GUARD: You know the drill.

JO and LEE stand against the wall. VIV doesn't move.

VIV: This one. Tried to attack me. Stopped them. I stopped them. The others, they didn't help. Please. You've got to let me go now. I helped. Did I pass the test?

The door opens.

GUARD: Get against the wall. Hands where I can see them.

VIV: But I helped! I stopped them! They were going to kill us all!

GUARD: *(To VIV)* Not you. *(To CAL)* You. Against the wall.

CAL: But I...

VIV: That's right. I knew I was right. Never trust, never, it was a test, right?

The GUARD has walked into the middle of the cell, picked up the wrist restraints.

GUARD: *(To VIV)* Turn around.

VIV: What, no... I...

The GUARD forcibly turns VIV around, secures their wrists. Goes to pick up the blindfold/bag.

VIV: No, please, please I- Help me! Please help me!

CAL, LEE and JO look at each other, awkward.

JO: It's no good.

LEE: Do as they say.

JO: No point fighting.

The GUARD places the bag/blindfold over VIV's eyes.

GUARD: That's right. No point fighting. Downstairs for you.

VIV struggles as the GUARD leads them out of the door.

VIV: No! I didn't, it wasn't me... please!

The door slams and the others turn to look at each other.

CAL: Thank you.

LEE: It's ok. There really was no saving Viv.

JO: Viv?

LEE: Their name. It was Viv.

JO: Come on, sit down. They'll bring food soon.

LEE: Good. Hungry.

TIME PASSES. It's as if someone has pressed fast-forward. This can be represented through a series of tableaux, through movement and soundscape. The three become closer. When time slows down again, they are sitting on the floor laughing.

CAL: SNAP!

JO: *(Laughing)* How can you possibly tell?! There's no cards!

LEE: Can't you see? They played two sixes! You played a six, then they played a six. Obvious.

JO: I didn't even know it was snap, I thought we were playing snakes and ladders!

CAL: That finished HOURS ago!

LEE: HOURS!

They all laugh.

JO: Idiots.

The laughter is halted by footsteps, keys, a shutter.

GUARD: You know the routine.

LEE, JO and CAL all stand facing the wall. GUARD enters.

Beat.

GUARD: Come on.

LEE: What?

GUARD: Time to go.

CAL: All of us?

GUARD: All of you. Moving out. Congratulations.

JO: But...

CAL and LEE hug.

CAL: I can't believe it.

LEE: Me neither. *(To JO)* We're getting out, moving on. Can you believe it?

GUARD: One at a time. No funny business.

GUARD indicates the open door DSC, LEE and CAL eagerly run through it and stand/sit in the audience.

LEE: Come on!

CAL: Come on Jo, we're moving on!

JO: I…

GUARD: This again?

JO: I think I'll stay. Not ready yet.

GUARD: It might be years.

CAL: What're you doing?

LEE: Come on!

JO: Mum always said I could never make decisions…

GUARD: Your choice.

The door slams. Keys turn in the lock. JO stands, looking at the door. Slowly, they push a crate up to the window and stare out.

JO: So bright. Safer in here.

JO sits on the crate.

JO: You are my sunshine. My only sunshine. You make me happy, when skies are grey. You'll never know dear, how much I love you… You are my sunshine, in every way.

TWO ACTING EXERCISES

There follows two short scenes that will be useful in lessons about given circumstances, character motivations and conflict.

Both are duologues, with characters only referred to as 'A' and 'B'. The exercise should run something like this:

a) Ask volunteers to read through the scenes for the rest of the group. Often, particularly with the first one, students may make comments like "Nothing much is happening." Other groups may suggest what is happening in each.
b) Describe how the performance of each scene can be changed dramatically through different GIVEN CIRCUMSTANCES, different CONFLICT and MOTIVATIONS.
c) Split the group into pairs – if you have an odd number the second scene can be performed with 'B' being split into two characters.
d) As they read through the scenes, give each pair their given circumstances and INDIVIDUALLY give each performer their want or motivation. This can be done most easily with pre-preparing slips of paper.
e) Give the students time to rehearse their scenes.
f) Watch each scene and discuss how changing motivations and adding given circumstances can completely change a scene and an actor's performance. It is the job of an actor to make decisions based on the information provided by the text, to bring a text to life.
g) If there is time, ask the students to come up with their own given circumstances and motivations and perform some examples.

Scene 1

A: Can I make you some tea?

B: Tea?

A: Yes.

Beat.

B: Go on then.

Beat. A stirs the pot and pours, watching B.

A: Here.

B: Thank you.

They drink.

A: Good?

B: Yes thanks.

A: I'm glad we've found some time for this talk.

B: Me too.

Beat.

A: Sugar?

B: No thanks.

Beat. They drink.

A: Biscuit?

B: That's ok, I've got some chocolate digestives here.

B reaches in their bag for the biscuits, pulls out a packet and offers them to A.

B: Would you like one?

A: Yes, I will.

A takes one.

A: Delicious.

B: Yes. Aren't they?

A: Yes.

Silence. They look at each other.

Scene 1 – Given Circumstances / Wants

TEACHER NOTE: Given circumstances should be shared with the pair. Individual wants only shared with each performer. These are only suggestions: an extension would be to let the students come up with their own.

1

Given circumstances: A and B are married.

A wants B to drink the tea, because A has poisoned it.

B knows A has poisoned the tea, so is pretending to drink it and is looking for the first chance to escape.

2

Given Circumstances: A is a criminal and B is a detective trying to catch them.

A wants to escape.

B wants A to confess. B thinks some evidence is in a back room of the house.

3

Given Circumstances: A and B have been dating for 2 years.

A is building up the courage to ask B to marry them.

B is building up the courage to tell A it's over.

Scene 2

A wood.

A: This is the spot.

B: Right here?

A: Yep.

B: Ok, so what next – shall I pitch the tent or go and get some firewood?

A: They both sound excellent ideas.

B: But... what will you be doing?

A: I'll be here.

Pause.

B: What if there's wild animals?

A: Here, take this whistle. If anything... jumps out at you, give it a quick toot and I'll come running.

B: If anything what?

A: You'll be fine.

B: And you'll be...

A: I'll be right here. You get the wood and I...

B: You can put the tent up?

A: That's exactly right. I'll put the tent up.

B starts to leave, then turns.

B: You'll be here? When I get back?

A: I'll be here, yes.

Tiny beat.

A: Putting the tent up.

B: Good.

A: See you then.

B: Yep... bye.

They look at each other.

Scene 2 Given Circumstances / Wants

1

Given Circumstances: A is an 'adventure coordinator', B has paid to go on a survival weekend in the woods.

A: Has been given the job by mistake and knows nothing about survival. Wants B to think they know what they're doing.

B: B wants to stay or wants A to come with them.

2

Given Circumstances: A is the child of B.

A: Wants B to leave so they can have an adventure on their own.

B: Doesn't want to leave their child in the forest but wants to be a 'cool' parent.

3

Given Circumstances: A and B are friends but have had a massive argument. They have both been upset by it.

A: Wants B to apologise.

B: Wants A to apologise.

Romeo and Juliet Extract

This is a great introduction to the play for English and drama students.

Pupils will need to be given some background before starting, mainly they'll need to know about the long-standing animosity between the two families.

For drama students, this is also an opportunity for them to work on staging a scene using TABLEAUX and MORPHING (Bringing tableaux to life or moving from one tableau to another). It is also an opportunity to teach the students some basic stage combat under carefully supervised conditions. Make sure they are performing the moves safely before allowing them to use them.

The key here is to encourage students to create a scene of violence and chaos, without it really becoming uncontrolled. Teachers should encourage students to think about the timing of the piece so that the ruler (so called so they can be played by any gender) is heard and the fighting stops completely on cue to hear their final speech. Teachers should also encourage students to think about where they want their audience and when the class watches the piece, discuss how successful they have been in clearly presenting the story.

ROMEO AND JULIET (6 actors)

A hot, dusty street in Verona. The Montagues frozen in a tableau that gradually comes to life.

MONTAGUE1: Quarrel, I will back thee.

MONTAGUE2: By my head, here come the Capulets.

MONTAGUE3: By my heel, I care not.

The Capulets enter. The enemies circle each other. Montagues bite their thumbs.

CAPULET1: Do you bite your thumb at us sir?

MONTAGUE3: I do bite my thumb, sir.

CAPULET2: A word with one of you...

MONTAGUE1: Just a word? Couple it with something, make it a word, and a blow.

CAPULET3: Do you quarrel sir?

MONTAGUE2: Quarrel sir? No sir.

CAPULET1: Draw, if you be men!

They fight. This can be in slow motion, with moments of quicker action, accompanied with sound that grows louder – insults or just noises, grunts, be imaginative with your voices.

MONTAGUE2: Part, fools! Put up your swords, you know not what you do.

CAPULET2: Turn thee, Benvolio, look upon thy death.

MONTAGUE2: I do but keep the peace, put up thy sword.

CAPULET3: What, drawn and talk of peace? I hate the word as I hate hell, all Montagues and thee.

More fighting that builds to a climax. At the height of the conflict, Montague 3 becomes the ruler and bellows the following lines. The other characters look suitably guilty.

Ruler: Rebellious subjects, enemies to peace, if ever you disturb our streets again, your lives shall pay the forfeit of the peace. Once more, on pain of death, all men depart!

Montagues and Capulets exit.

Printed in Dunstable, United Kingdom